Praise for Pegine and Bragging Rights

"Pegine Echevarria is honest -- and, sometimes, brutally so. I say that in praise, because in today's world of generic authors offering bland advice, 'Bragging Rights' will a shock to your system. My bet is that it's one you -- and I -- need to take our team's performance to a higher level. Don't just buy the book...devour it! You are only twenty-one days away from transformed teams."

> **SCOTT MCKAIN** - author of three Amazon.com #1 business bestsellers; including *"Collapse of Distinction"* named by thirty major newspapers as one of the top ten business books of 2009; and, member of the Professional Speakers Hall of Fame

"'Bragging Rights' is a must read for all managers. It will not only shorten the curve for success but it will ensure continual growth for each member of the team. Reality 101... Pegine tells it like it is, which is refreshing and rewarding. By embracing the ideas from this book, managers will uncover all the things they are doing right and discover better ways of doing things to maximize their transformation as an both an individual, employee and manager."

> **JIMMY CABRERA,** CSP – One of Hispanic Business Magazines Top Ten Motivational Speaker, Consultant, and author of *"What's in your Backpack?"*

"A standing ovation for Pegine. This book is entertaining, full of great ideas, packed with how to information, it will make your team's productivity go through the roof if you apply its principles."

> **DR. JOACHIM DE POSADA,** Author of the world wide best seller, *"Don't Eat the Marshmallow Yet...The Secret to Sweet Success in Work and Life".*

"Pegine has done it again! She has given managers a straight forward formula for maximizing their own leadership abilities and the potential of the teams they lead. A must read for those who want to reach the next level."

> **TAMMY EDWARDS**, Director - Inclusion & Diversity, Sprint

"Don't think twice - just buy this book and put it to work for your team. These techniques and strategies work in small teams and large. You'll see the difference immediately!"

> **DALE COLLIE**, retired Army major Named by Fast Company magazine as one of America's Top 50 innovative leaders Author of *Winning under Fire: Turn Stress into Success the US Army Way*

"Leadership doesn't come from your title of 'boss' or 'manager' it comes from within us. Pegine's message of self examination first is critical to the growth of

everyone else on your team. I wish all managers would read 'Bragging Rights' because the book gives you the insight and the tools to see your people differently – appealing to your ability to see the best of your people and their capabilities through your own self examination"

ROBIN WAHBY, Senior Partner, New York Life

"HR departments, Division heads, CEO's should buy this book for their managers because 'Bragging Rights' makes one realize the true meaning of a successful team and recognizes what makes the new entrepreneurial generation want and choose to stay part of your organization. Pegine is an experienced professional whose candor and no-nonsense style communicates the core issues of any successful team – the emotions and human characteristics involved with success, results and community."

DIANNE B. DEVITT, CMP, CEO/President, The DND Group.

"Pegine has done it again! What an awesome book. In her inimitable style Pegine has taken the essence of team building and put it in an approach and style that can be followed by any supervisor or manager wanting to create the dynamics of a team. The approach and insights are amazing as they get to the very core of how our work mates think and act. As managers and consultants we all believe this will lead to results far above the workplace norms. Get it and apply it – TODAY."

GRAEME NICHOL, CEO, OPM Solutions

"Take a look at your calendar. What day is 21 days from today? With this book you can have a fully engaged and productive team by THAT day, literally. The team of your dreams could be only three weeks from you right now. Let Pegine Echevarria guide you through the simple process of shifting your thoughts and actions into a vein of pure productivity. You'll enjoy the journey and then you can claim Bragging Rights, or let your team do it. By the way, whether you do or don't that date is still fast approaching. Start reading now!"

JIM CATHCART, bestselling author of *The Acorn Principle & Relationship Selling*

"As an executive coach, I look for tools for managers to become better team leaders. Pegine, your book Bragging Rights, Transform Your Team in 21 Days is chock full of great tools and lays out a winning plan. Managers and their teams will flourish when they follow your simple, daily instructions for the 21 days. Thank you!!"

DOUG WILDER- Wilder Business Success, Inc.-
Building your people and building your self

"Unless your team is already perfect, 'Bragging Rights' is sure to help get you there! Pegine does a magnificent job of combining real-world scenarios, detailed coaching and strategies, useful tips, and positive reinforcements in way any manager or team leader can easily follow. Add the humorous tone, skilled insights, and interactive assignments to foster long-term retention of the material, and you have one of the most effective team improvement resources ever written. This book goes way beyond team building!"

MARK GOLDWICH, Owner, Gold Star Adjusters, and author of *"Uncovered - What Really Happens After the Storm, Flood, Earthquake or Fire".*

"Bragging Rights gives managers a formula for how do get more productivity from their team in 21 days. It is not theory. It is a roll up our sleeves and let's get down to it program that will get buy in from your team and produce results. It will help take your team from where they are to where they can be."

CHIP EICHELBERGER, Sales motivational speaker

"If your organization is in need of a burst of energy from a dynamic and extremely engaging speaker, Pegine is your person! Pegine is a powerhouse in understanding the art of communication and diversity and how it relates to your employees and ultimately your bottom line. Be sure to hold on to your seats and prepare for an awesome ride with Pegine!"

TANYA STEWART, Consultant/Principal at The Smith Stewart Solutions Group

"If you're in a position of leadership or aspire to be -- do yourself a favor and buy a copy of Bragging Rights *by Pegine Echavarria. It will be an investment you make in yourself which will pay for itself many times over. What you learn will enable you to create powerful team environments. Pegine has packed in the solid advice in this book. Well done Pegine!"*

JOSH HINDS, Speaker, Author, and Entrepreneurial Educator. www.JoshHinds.com Founder of the world's largest motivation website www.GetMotivation.com

"Pegine Echevarria is one of the most powerful business growth experts on the planet, and this book shows why! I recommend you read this book and share it with your team, and people in your network! You will be glad you did!!!!!"

WILLIE JOLLEY, Best Selling Author of *"A Setback Is A Setup For A Comeback"* and *"An Attitude of Excellence!"*

ISBN: 978-0-9839791-1-1

Printed in the United States of America
First Edition

Transform Your Team

in *21* Days

Bragging Rights

Play Big Pegine

PEGINE ECHEVARRIA
MSW, CSP

This is your night! You are all decked out and your team is excited. People are dressed up. Someone is wearing black sequins to the event. The team is excited because all of their work is paying off.

You are smiling as you reflect on the last few months. The team wasn't performing at their best and you knew something had to change. Who knew that when you started the process you would be the change agent. Changing what you did changed what they did.

Black sequins on the cover represent the night you achieve your Bragging Rights.

Bragging Rights!

I work with thousands of managers, supervisors, senior leaders and entrepreneurs; all with deadlines, missions, and goals. These men and women know what they want to achieve as managers and leaders; however, they have faced the reality that they can't realize their goals alone – they need their team.

Of course, knowing you need help to achieve your goal and GETTING the help are two different things.

This is my world.

My company, Team Pegine Inc. motivates leaders in a diverse world. We work with managers and leaders in the US Navy, US Army, US Coast Guard and in companies like Harley Davidson, Verizon, Colgate Palmolive and Intel. We also work with leaders in direct sales who manage large teams of people and who have to continually motivate their teams in a very diverse, global world.

Time and time again I hear them struggle with "How do I manage and motive my team for mission success?" or "I don't have the time to deal with all the drama!" and, finally – "There has GOT TO BE A BETTER WAY!"

I wrote Bragging Rights after hearing from managers

and leaders encouraging me to write about the process; I wrote the book for them, their colleagues and for you.

The book is about people (you) managing people (them).

If you knew me, you would know that I don't mess around. I love reading and hate wasting time going through the fluff in leadership books when what I want is – the author to tell me what to do! This is a tell it like it is book. It is action-oriented. It is tactics.

It is a stop complaining – get on with it – move forward – leadership book.

I want you to earn your bragging rights.

I want you to hear from your team, "YOU ROCK!"

I want you to attend an awards ceremony having someone in black sequins congratulate you on your team's outstanding results.

Like you, I don't do this alone.

The team behind Team Pegine Inc. is like a well-oiled machine – purring along and moving forward. Two key leaders within my organization are Tamara Goldwich and David Herbin. They have been with me since the very beginning. They are amazing; they go above and beyond to ensure mission success at headquarters and for our clients.

We have an incredible support staff who make us look good, connect cheerfully with clients, ensure that we have mission success, and they are most appreciated (thanks everyone!)

We provide speakers and trainers throughout the country. They are first class all the way – Dale Collie, Paul Mottola, Eileen McDargh, Kirsten Arnold are just some of our incredible speakers who give our clients outstanding results.

Our team includes incredible consultants, partners and vendors who allow us to be rock stars! Dana Bussiere, Joe Tee, and Lana Milakovich, among others.

Finally, my mastermind group – who makes managing teams look effortless. Thanks for the kick in the butt – Anna Lopez Brosche, Teresa Myers, and Ann Sabbag.

INTRODUCTION

People don't defend ...
or protect ...
what they don't own.

This is a book about ownership .... about helping your people move from a "What do *they* want?" mindset to a "What do I want?" mindset. A "What do I want?" mindset is the only mindset where breakthrough performance, for teams and individuals, can take place.

When you, the manager, are the only one who owns someone else's outcome, your job is impossible.

When your team members own their own jobs, their own processes, and their own outcomes, your job as a manager becomes easy.

Have you ever heard yourself saying (or thinking) things like the following?

"Mike, my sales guy, is a whiner. He complains all the time and is constantly finding fault with other people's ideas."

"Aisha, our research specialist, isn't really a team player. She seems to be distracted easily during team meetings, and I always get the feeling that she can't wait for the meeting to be over."

"Dave, the office manager, has no follow-through. He talks a mile a minute about what other people ought to do, but he never actually executes anything himself."

"Juan, our copywriter, has really got to learn to pay attention to details. He's one of these people who talks a good game, but he misses basic writing errors. Yesterday, a press release he wrote went out with a very embarrassing typo. My boss gave me hell about it."

Sometimes, we managers think: *Why can't people simply DO the things they're supposed to do? Why don't they make SOME effort to improve?*

And yet ...

What would you say if I told you that Mike, Aisha, Dave, and Juan were *all giving you clues right now* about how they could transform their performance ... focus relentlessly on adding real value to the organization ... and help you move to the next level in your own career?

What would you say if I told you that *the very performance problems you spotted* were signals to you about workplace triumphs Mike, Aisha, Dave, and Juan were ready and eager to make happen, starting tomorrow morning ... triumphs they would take personal accountability for delivering, and would brag about to anyone who would listen?

This book is based on principles I've used to turn teams around at some of America's most prestigious companies –

and also at the US Army Corps of Engineers, the Army National Guard, and the Army. If you are a manager, I wrote this book for you.

My premise is that the people you supervise can only increase their value to the company a) if you, the manager, know where your people's true skills lie and give them "bragging rights" on how they deploy those skills; and b) if you, the manager, make a personal commitment to growth and change.

If a) and b) are not in place right now (and they're not in place, in my experience, in most American workplaces), then your team members *don't own their outcomes* (you do), and they can't possibly give you their best, *because they don't yet know what their best is.*

DAY 1:

"Why Do I Have To Do This?"

"Why can't my people see what they are capable of on their own?"

"What is so complicated about meeting a target that is set out clearly in a job description?"

"What is so difficult about doing X? I used to do it with no problem."

"Why can't they follow basic instructions? I told them clearly and calmly, and with as much positive energy as I can manage, exactly

what I want done and when I want it completed
– what else do they want?"

"Why do I have to get all touchy-feely to get people to
actually do anything around here?"

"Why is this my job and not the employee's job? Don't they
know what's in their own job description?"

"Why is it my job to motivate them? Didn't we hire people
who are capable of motivating themselves?"

"What am I supposed to do – baby sit the person?"

"Why the @$#%& do I have to do this?"

These are the kinds of initial questions I hear from managers when I train this program in person.

Often, they are sitting in the training room because someone else suggested, or perhaps mandated, that they show up for the day and listen to what I had to say. If you are reading these words right now, not because you want to, but because someone else asked you to read this book, it is possible similar questions may be running through your mind right now.

In answer to these questions, I can only offer a single, stark, and unassailable fact: Sometimes, when our teams do things that drive us nuts, that's a signal of how we need to grow as managers.

That's a tough lesson, and it's not one we always want to focus on. But if we want to improve our teams, and move our own careers to the next level, it's a lesson we've got to learn.

If we keep on doing what we are doing right now with our team, we can guarantee ourselves that we will get exactly the same results. So if you are happy with the results you are getting from your team, there is no need to move forward with the content in this book.

If, on the other hand, you have a sense that there is room for improvement ...

... that your team should be spending less time backbiting and politicking, and more time focused on productive activities ...

... that your team is capable of doing great things if only they could focus on the business at hand and break through some distracting habits and preconceptions . . .

... if any of these ring true for you as you assess your team and its performance in a real world, read on. And don't worry. This won't hurt. It will actually be fun!

Point to ponder: **The person you allow to make you angry is the person who controls you.**

Each of your team members has value ... even if you, because you're human, choose to focus on the negative aspects that you see in a team member's performance.

Think of a person on your staff. Now consider the answers to these questions before you move on in this chapter.

- Is this person valued by you?
- If so, for what is the person valued?
- How do you communicate that value?

Just as you see things that you want to change in your employees, they see things that they would like to change in you. *No growth in your team is possible without a parallel commitment to personal growth from you, the manager.*

Point to ponder: **You will only win when your team wins.**

To make this book work for you, you'll need two things: A notebook and commitment.

Each day, you'll use the commitment to read the short chapter that connects to that day ... and complete the written exercise in your notebook. Today, your assignment couldn't be simpler: Write *one-sentence* answers to the three questions that appear at the end of this chapter.

Again: Why should you bother with this?

Well, if you're interested in this topic at all, my guess is that there's at least one, and possibly as many as six, specific reasons for that interest. Typically, those reasons are:

- Somebody told you or asked you to read the book. (Okay – you're doing this because your boss wants you to see what's between these covers. But why? In all likelihood, your boss wants you to read this book because of one of the following five challenges.)

- High potential within you and your team.
- Low productivity on your team.
- Low morale on your team.
- High turnover on your team.
- High recruitment costs.

If *any one* of these things is true in your situation, that means something has to change. And guess what? Just reading these words isn't *enough* change. Something *you as a manager are doing* has to change.

So we need to begin to get comfortable with analyzing where we have been and what we have been doing. We can't change our people without being honest and up-front with ourselves about what's actually happening on the ground.

This book challenges you to be honest with yourself. It challenges you to look in the mirror and say, loud enough so you yourself can actually hear it, "Hey, what's happening with my team? And what part did I play in what's happening right now?"

The three questions below are designed to help you begin the process of seeking your own responsibility in the job of developing an atmosphere where people feel totally comfortable communicating value to each other, an atmosphere where everyone is equipped, empowered, and motivated to communicate his or her value to their superiors. *If that's not what's already happening,* (and usually it isn't), you will need to do a little self-assessment *if and only if you want to get something out of this process.*

Ready?

Pull out your notebook!

IN ONE SENTENCE, how would you describe the value your team adds to the organization as a whole? (In other words, if your boss sat down with you this afternoon and told you that your department was about to be eliminated, effective tomorrow morning, unless you came up with a single good reason to keep it, what reason would you give?)

Bragging Rights!

IN ONE SENTENCE, when was the last time you sat down for a coaching meeting with one of your team members? (Be as specific as you can with the date.)

IN ONE SENTENCE, describe what prompted the meeting. (Was the coaching meeting scheduled or impromptu? Who initiated the meeting? Was the meeting part of a formal salary review session?)

⇥ ⇤

Do not move on to Day 2 today,
or any other day in this book.

Complete the short written assignment (above)
in your notebook before you continue.

DAY 2:

The Meeting Both People Wish They Could Skip

Performance review time.

Joe, a five-year employee at components giant ACIWW[1], is trying once again to read his supervisor's mind: "What, exactly, does he want from me?" He's been worrying about this meeting for weeks.

---

1 ACIWW – A company I worked with that wants to remain anonymous.

He's not the only one.

Ed, Joe's manager, doesn't really know what he wants from Joe. He's uncomfortable discussing things he can't quantify with numbers, he's worried about his own upcoming performance review, he's afraid of saying something that will get him in trouble, and he's uncertain where Joe's potential for growth really lies.

Instead of asking questions that will help Joe develop a personal goal that will build on the best of what he has accomplished over the last three months, and *how* he personally has accomplished it, Ed takes the easy way out. He starts a discussion about workplace *processes*, skipping over Joe as a person.

After all, evaluating processes is what Ed is good at.

Process analyses during performance reviews, however, drive employees like Joe nuts.

The result? Joe nods his head obediently, takes notes, then retreats to his cubicle, where he mutters unflattering things about his boss.

One personnel evaluation at a time, ACIWW's historic commitment to innovation and improvement is collapsing.

In thousands upon thousands of America's companies, collaboration and teamwork are the exception. And silence – specifically, covering yourself to avoid punishment from above – is the rule.

Many (though not all) of ACIWW's numbers-driven managers have lost sight of the entrepreneurial vision that launched the company in the first place. What's more, a fair number of these managers aren't particularly good at – and don't really enjoy – communicating with the people who report to them. (In fact, the majority of managers I train have never asked their direct reports about what they do in their leisure time.)

Point to ponder: **What your people do *outside* of the workplace may illustrate talents and connections they could be using *inside* the workplace.**

The result of this habitual distance between manager and employee is a three-part crisis undermining the company's return on its human resource investment.

1. Loss of organizational opportunity. Good ideas that are developed by individual employees are rarely shared throughout the organization because managers don't hear about them in the first place.

2. Loss of personal productivity. When managers don't even know which workers are posting personal increases in productivity, or why, they can't encourage these behaviors over time.

3. Loss of team cohesion. Many team members follow Joe's example, investing lots of energy in a performance review process that ultimately frustrates them. They form unrealistic ideas and expectations of management, but end up demotivated and cynical, and then clam up about what, exactly, they're doing all day long. People often conclude – correctly – that their manager simply has no idea what he or she wants. They form cliques and spend too much time on things like backbiting and politicking.

Does any of this sound familiar?

Pull out your notebook!

1. How do I currently evaluate employee performance?

2. What, specifically, do I measure during performance evaluation?

3. Exactly how often do evaluations take place?

4. What kind of information (if any) do employees provide to me before the evaluation? (Be specific.)

5. What kind of information (if any) do employees provide to me after the evaluation? (Again, be specific.)

6. How would you assess the way your team members feel about the performance evaluation system that's currently in place? (Be honest. You might as well, because no one is going to read your answers except you.)

7. Write down the names of each of your direct reports on the left-hand side of a blank sheet of paper.

8. Now, on the right-hand side of that same piece of paper, write down everything you know about what that person does *outside* the workplace.

Bragging Rights!

Do not move on to Day 3 today,
or any other day in this book.

Complete the short written assignment (above)
in your notebook before you continue.

DAY 3:

"What They Want, What I Want"

B ack to our story...

ACIWW was still an industry leader within its primary market. The company's historic emphasis on innovation and creativity, however, had declined.

ACIWW was certainly not alone in this regard. In many of today's large companies, managers, employees and team members must contend with a cover-your-anatomy mentality that leads to a toxic workplace culture. In this kind of environment, people generally refuse to take risks or talk openly about their ideas for making things better.

Point to ponder: **When innovation and creativity decline at the team level, they also decline at the organizational level.**

My job, as the consultant ACIWW hired to work with employees, was to answer a simple question: Why?

Here's what I found out. In their interactions with managers, employees were focusing on avoiding mentioning anything that might conceivably lead to a "black mark" on quarterly performance evaluations.

In other words, most team members were, like their managers, in cover-your-anatomy mode, which usually meant confirming the assumptions of managers. In many cases, this meant that managers did not get a full picture of the true accomplishments, assets, or requirements of their team members.

ACIWW's ability to support high-functioning, innovative teams had been undercut. Poor morale, mediocre daily plans, and unproductive, low-information communication patterns were daily workplace norms.

I had to work with the team at ACIWW to develop tools to help them *identify and promote their own value as a regular workplace event ... not just during annual performance evaluations.*

I helped the people at ACIWW to move from a "What do *THEY* want" mindset to a "What do *I* want" mindset.

I helped them step away from the question, "What do *THEY* want me to be within this organization?" to this question:

"What do I want to be within the organization ... and how can I help the organization be what it wants to be?"

The only way to do that is to get people to know their own value ... and the value of others in their world. And we as managers can't do that if we don't know, or can't easily articulate, what kind of value the person is currently delivering.

Bragging Rights!

Pull out your notebook!

On the following pages, make a list of all the team members who report to you ... and describe YOUR PER-SPECTIVE on the value that each team member adds to the organization as a whole.

Focus ONLY on positive value added, even if you have problems with the person in question.

⊩⊨ ⊨⊩

Do not move on to Day 4 today,
or any other day in this book.

Complete the short written assignment (above)
in your notebook before you continue.

DAY 4:

The Starter Form

Based on the work you did in Day 3...

Fill out the following "Starter Form" for EACH of your team members. If you have one person who reports to you, fill out the form for one person. If you have two people who report to you, fill out the form for two people. If you have 60 people who report to you, fill out the form for 60 people.

Bragging Rights!

Important – fill out only the first three columns. Leave the column on the far right-hand side blank for now.

Team member's name:_____

3 things I couldn't do if you weren't here.	3 strengths you bring to this job.	3 reasons I want you to stick around.	What do you want to be within the organization and how can you help the organization be what it wants to be?

I realize this may look a little weird. Please do it anyway. You're going to use this form as a point of entry for a private, one-on-one session with EACH of your team members. You're going to share ONLY POSITIVE things during that meeting ... and you're going to give your team member a "Homework Assignment" for ONE WEEK FROM TODAY. The assignment is going to be to fill in that far right-hand column. (Obviously, you will be responsible for filling in the information in the other columns.)

Point to ponder: **If you only share what's *not* working and what you *don't* value, your team will develop a cover-your-anatomy work culture.**

You will soon (not today) be scheduling a one-on-one meeting with your team member that demonstrates you are willing to celebrate his or her value. Filling out the form in this chapter is the beginning of that process.

Pull out your notebook!

IMPORTANT: KEEP ALL OF THE INFORMATION BELOW TO YOURSELF. DO NOT SHARE THE ANSWERS WITH ANYONE WHO REPORTS TO YOU.

(For each team member:) Where, specifically, would you most like to see this person improve in terms of work performance?

(For each team member:) What do you think is a realistic short-term career goal for this person?

(For each team member:) What do you think is a realistic long-term career goal for this person?

(For each team member:) What THREE communication mistakes do you think it's possible you could have made with this person up to this point? (This could be an active mistake – as in accusing the person of doing something improper that he or she didn't really do – or a passive mistake – as in not meeting with the person regularly to go over performance and coaching issues.)

+≥ ≤+

Do not move on to Day 5 today,
or any other day in this book.

Complete the short written assignment (above)
in your notebook before you continue.

Using The Starter Form

Pick ONE AND ONLY ONE of your team members. This is the team member you will be focusing on for this chapter.

Based on the work you did on Day 4...

First: Select the ONE MOST FLATTERING response you filled out for this individual team member under the heading **Three things I couldn't do if you weren't here.**

In private, when you are all alone, and OUT LOUD, practice saying this about your employee, as though he or she were in the room. In other words, pick out the single most flattering (from the employee's point of view) thing that you, the manager, could not possibly accomplish if the person weren't here. (Example: If the person handles phone traffic for your organization, you might consider saying, "I just want you to know that we couldn't possibly keep track of all the phone inquiries we get here on a daily basis without you.")

Second: Pick out the MOST OBVIOUS response you filled out for this individual team member under the heading **Three strengths you bring to this job.**

Point to ponder: **If you don't take the initiative to practice what you will say ahead of time, your interactions during this meeting will slip back into your "default" mode with this employee.**

In private, when you are all alone, and OUT LOUD, practice saying this about your employee, as though he or she were in the room. In other words, pick out the single most obvious strength this team member possesses, and practice acknowledging it in real, spoken words. WARN-ING: This strength may or may not be the one you noticed first when you decided to hire this person! The objective here is to practice mentioning the strength that this employee is most likely to recognize about himself or herself already. (Example: If the person displays a lot of energy and resilience when handling the phones for your company, you might consider saying, "I hope you know that I appreciate the incredible amount of energy and drive you bring to your job, and the stamina you show on a long shift. My feeling is that your last hour of the day is just about as strong as your first hour of the day, and that's remarkable.")

Third: Based on what you know now about this person – whether that's a lot or a little – pick out the MOST PERSUASIVE response you filled out for this individual team member under the heading **Three reasons I want you to stick around.**

In private, when you are all alone, and OUT LOUD, practice saying this about your employee, as though he or she were in the room. The idea here is to pick the reason the employee – not you – would consider most compelling as a reason to stay on the job. (Example: If the person is strongly oriented toward team and family, has emerged as an important member of the team, and has close ties to others in the work group, you might consider saying, "Since we hired you three months ago, you've made some very important contributions to the team – so important, in fact, that I've noticed that the other people on the team have come to depend on you. I have, too, and that's one reason why I really want you to stick around.")

MAKE SURE YOU PRACTICE SAYING EXPLICITLY THAT YOU WANT THIS PERSON TO STAY ON THE TEAM.

Pull out your notebook!

ANSWER THE FOLLOWING QUESTIONS IN YOUR WORKBOOK <u>AFTER</u> YOU HAVE PRACTICED SAYING, OUT LOUD AND IN PRIVATE, THE THREE ITEMS MENTIONED IN THIS CHAPTER.

Do you see any connections – even indirect connections – between the positive things you have identified and the areas where you would most like to see this person improve in terms of work performance? What are they?

What workplace strengths does this person possess that connect to your short-term career goal for this person? (Be specific.)

What workplace strengths does this person possess that connect to your long-term career goal for this person? (Be specific.)

Bragging Rights!

Do not move on to Day 6 today,
or any other day in this book.

Complete the short written assignment (above)
in your notebook before you continue.

DAY 6:

The Challenge

Here's where it gets interesting!

Today, my challenge to you is to *hold* this brief meeting with each of your direct reports. Here are the ground rules:

- You may only skip this meeting if you are *actively* pursuing termination proceedings against this employee. Otherwise ... get face to face, in private.

- The meeting must last for no more than ten minutes per employee. (Five is better.)
- The meeting must focus *only* on positive things that you value about this employee. No criticism or suggestions on how this person might improve his or her performance.
- No, really. I'm serious. You must make *absolutely no* direct or indirect criticism of the employee or his or her performance during this meeting.
- The meeting must end with you giving a copy of the Starter Form to the employee. The copy you hand over should have your handwritten work in the first three columns, and its right-hand column should be left blank.
- The employee's homework is to complete that fourth column and return the form to you no later than one week from today.

Go for it!

Point to ponder: **If you don't radically change the way you communicate with your employees, you can't expect to bring about radical changes in performance.**

Pull out your notebook!

ANSWER THE FOLLOWING QUESTIONS IN YOUR WORKBOOK FOR EACH EMPLOYEE ON YOUR TEAM AFTER YOU HAVE CONDUCTED THIS MEETING.

1. What, in your view, was the high point in the meeting?
2. What, in your view, was the low point of the meeting?
3. What would you have done differently?

Bragging Rights!

*Do not move on to Day 7 today,
or any other day in this book.*

*Complete the short written assignment (above)
in your notebook before you continue.*

DAY 7:

Two Missing Pieces

D id you have the meetings with your team members? Did you share the Starter Form with each of them? If so, great. If not, don't continue with this book until you do this exercise.

You are still not ready to conduct a performance evaluation, even though you now know exactly why you want the person to stay. You are missing two essential pieces of the puzzle.

Bragging Rights!

Point to ponder: **You have now laid the foundation for positive change. But the foundation is not the whole building.**

You do not yet know where you are in terms of your own growth and development as a manager.

And you do not know what your employee's "sweet spot" is – what he or she is temperamentally *already inclined to do well.*

Days 8 through 11 will be all about identifying your own pattern of growth and development as a manger. These are incredibly important days, and I am going to urge you once again not to skip them, but instead to read them carefully and to complete all the associated written exercises.

Days 12 through 20 will be all about identifying, not just what you want your employee to accomplish, but what he or she is already *predisposed* to accomplish at a high level of proficiency. It sometimes startles managers to learn how very different their own expectations of their employees are from the true talents that these people possess. On these days, you will learn to identify what your employee does or could do that is likely to be superb . . . and you will learn how to begin a "positive feedback loop" by building your performance evaluation process around activities that connect to that core strength.

This idea is very exciting. In fact, it is so exciting that many managers with whom I work are tempted to skip over the material about their own development and outlook as a manager, and go directly to this "sweet spot" material so they can find out more about their employees' unexploited performance capacities.

Again: Don't skip days 8 through 11! Team growth *will not occur* without a commitment to your own personal growth as a manager. If your employees sense that you are not "walking the walk," it really does not matter how well you "talk the talk."

The final four chapters of the book, Days 18 through 21, will show you how to put it all together.

Pull out your notebook!

In your notebook, make a list of at least three managers you know (or knew) personally who had "congruence problems."

What I'm looking for is a list of at least three managers you reported to directly, worked with as a colleague, or met at least once who did not "walk the walk" after "talking the talk." I'm looking for managers in your life who had *stopped growing professionally* and who had some kind of *persistent communication problem with their team* as a result of that failure to grow. These should be managers who struck you as insincere, hypocritical, or exploitative in their outlook on work in general, and, if you reported to the person, in their outlook on your performance and contributions.

Once you have identified at least three such managers (it won't be hard), **write down at least one specific managerial trait from each person** that you are now committed to avoiding in your own career.

Do not move on to Day 8 today,
or any other day in this book.

Complete the short written assignment (above)
in your notebook before you continue.

DAY 8:

*The Managerial Growth Cycle
– The **Energetic** Phase*

When I started out as a manager in corporate America, I began at a point that I thought was unique – but turned out to be exactly the same place where most other managers begin their careers.

I realize now that, in the first phase of my development as a manager – and hey, maybe the first phase of yours – the key word was "inexperienced." I was so inexperienced that there were really only two assets I brought to the table: enthusiasm and energy!

<hr>

Point to ponder: **Sometimes managers don't know what they don't know.**

<hr>

Mind you, at the time, I *thought* I was bringing a lot more to the table than those two things. With hindsight, I realize now that enthusiasm and energy were the only things I had going at the time. I didn't have experience; I didn't have any contacts to speak of; and I certainly didn't have diplomacy.

My mindset when I first became a manager was dominated by a sense of absolute joy at having gotten the job at all – and a belief that very large amounts of energy and enthusiasm could solve any problem.

If only that were true!

At the time, I was thrilled to be involved at the managerial level; and I had no idea how much I didn't know about how to do my job. I believed that if I brought enough passion to any problem that landed on my desk, I'd be okay. I'd land on my feet, inspire my team with my sheer electrical wattage, and find the right answer, no matter what happened.

Why shouldn't I have believed that? Things were going *great*! There I was, in this wonderful new environment. I got to come into work every day and sit behind a desk that had a nameplate on it. I got to say my name over the phone – and follow it with an actual title that people would respect! What could be better than that? And what could possibly go wrong? I had been given an opportunity, and I knew that I wasn't the kind of person who squandered opportunities. All I had to do was to put enough energy into the job ... and surely I would get by.

Does this sound familiar, by any chance? Nowadays, when I share my very early management "philosophy" with participants in my training programs, I always see smiles and nods of recognition. At the time, though, I imagined that my belief in the transformative power of energy and enthusiasm was something very special that I alone brought to the job. As it turns out, it's the way *just about every manager* begins a managerial career.

In this early phase of the management growth cycle, we are fixated on one fact: we've moved up a notch! We don't know how much we don't know, but that's okay (we tell ourselves). We can improvise. So there we are, improvising, doing all the stuff that we find exciting – and then an interesting thing happens. We start learning about "the rules." We start learning about "how we do it here."

For many of us, this first phase of growth as a manager, the enthusiastic portion of the cycle, is a fairly short one. (For some people, it does not even last through the first day.) In my case, I burned through the enthusiasm piece fairly quickly and soon became just a little constricted with all of the advice and instructions, both spoken and unspoken, that I started to get.

Suddenly, I was getting all this information about what could and could not be done within the confines of my job as a manager.

Did anything like that happen to you?

Pull out your notebook!

In your notebook, make a list of at least three things that you *didn't know you didn't know* about managing people on your first day on the job as a manager.

Do not move on to Day 9 today,
or any other day in this book.

Complete the short written assignment (above)
in your notebook before you continue.

The Managerial Growth Cycle – The **Rebel** Phase

When I begin my training programs for managers, I play the song "Wild Thing" on the media device and crank up the volume to 11.

This instantly energizes the room and gets people focused on me as a trainer...because when I walk in, shaking and dancing and bobbing my head to the tune of that legendary anthem to nonconformity, people are wondering two things:

1. Who is this crazy woman? and
2. Where on earth is this going?

And that's fine. Those are two things that I want people to be thinking.

I don't use the song "Wild Thing" with its amplified power chords and badass "you move me" bridge, simply because I love the song. I use it because that attitude of rebelliousness is an important part of understanding – no, not the employee – but our own patterns of communication as a manager.

Believe it or not, "Wild Thing" is not a song about young love. It's really a song about *work*. It's about the way we look at our jobs!

It's about what happens in our heads when we walk in the door to work and a dozen different things hit us before we sit down at our desks. It's about the way we look at our job. It's about the way we process how we are going to get the items in our to-do list and our peoples' to-do lists checked off during the course of the day. It's about what we want to achieve and what we feel we have to do in order to get people involved with that achievement.

You know what? The song "Wild Thing" is also about you being in a meeting and hearing from your boss that you have some incredibly complex new initiative to pull off... and it's about you hearing yourself saying "yes" even though you are not entirely sure exactly how this is all going to happen. It's about what goes through your head when you look at your team members two minutes later and wonder, "How on earth am I going to get them to buy into this?"

Point to ponder: **After the "Enthusiasm" phase in the manager's career follows the "Rebellion" phase.**

"Wild Thing" is what happens after people try to sit you down and tell you "how we do things around here." It's the part of your managerial career where you think – or maybe even say – "Oh, yeah? Well that's not how *I* do it."

Many managers never move past the "Wild Thing" phase of their career. And that's a shame.

The bitter truth about the enthusiasm phase is that it almost always concludes with the new manager confronting a painful truth. Energy and enthusiasm *cannot* solve every problem. In order to succeed within an organization, we are told, you have to do it "our way." When we realize that that dictum really is meant to apply to us, we moved into another phase of our growth and development: that of the Rebel.

Rebel management says: "What you do outside of my zone is your business, but in here, we play by my rules ... and my rules alone. And if there's a problem, it's not because of me ... it's because of something *you* did, or something that happened Out There – probably something that The Man came up with to get me to conform. But *I* don't conform to anybody's rules but mine. I'm ... (power chord) ... *Wild Thing!*"

This is Rebel management in action. The problem is, this kind of thinking has a strange way of producing *employees* who insist on adopting a Rebel mindset no matter what you suggest to them.

When I was in the Rebellion mode, I didn't want to hear any lectures about the rules. I didn't want to follow the rules, or even learn how to live with them – I had to *change* the rules on my own terms. I wanted to buck the system ...

not because I knew where the system needed bucking, but because I didn't *understand* the system yet!

Typically, Rebel managers focus obsessively on what's *failing* or *might fail* in the system, and ignore what's actually *working* in the system. And they do the same thing to their people. They focus first and foremost on what's not working in someone's world, and they ignore what actually has been accomplished and what could be accomplished ... if they used the team's talents a little differently.

The Rebel is battling the rest of the world. It is not so much a "them against us" outlook ... as it is a "them against *me*" outlook.

Rebellion is all about identifying the flaws and mistakes of other people. It's all about finding reasons why it's *somebody else's fault* that you can't do X, Y, or Z.

That's a strange and hollow message to wrap your career around.

Isn't it?

"I told Jim exactly what to do – if he would just get off the dime and do it, we'd have no problems at all!"

"If I'd just had the right software for the sales team, we would have hit quota!"

"If we'd only stop merging with other companies, I could get the team to focus on its goals!"

"If only they would (fill in the blank) ..."

"I would (fill in the blank), if only ..."

The belief system of the Rebel manager is that something Out There, something that we don't control, is keeping us from attaining what we need to attain.

You know what else we believe when we're Rebels? We believe that if we complain loudly enough about the stuff that's happening Out There, a Fairy Godmother will suddenly materialize, touch us on the top of the head, make everybody behave, give us all the resources you need, and reassure us that a) everyone loves us and b) we don't have to change or grow.

- The reality is: We *do* have to change and grow as managers.

- The reality is: Managers are *always* dealing with challenges.
- The reality is: Things are *always* in flux.
- The reality is: We almost *never* get 100% of what we want from any situation.

In this second phase of our development as a manager, we dig our heels into the ground. We draw a line. We say, "Well, I am *never* going to do that." We say, "I may be getting a paycheck from this place, but I am not working for The Man. I am going to find a way to do things my way. Those may be your rules, but those are not the rules I am going to play by."

When somebody would come up to me and say something along the lines of, "Hey, we tried that ten years ago and it didn't work," the Rebel in me would come out. It did not really matter what I actually said with my mouth, the unspoken message was always the same in response to this warning: "Oh, yeah? Watch this. I'm going to change everything."

Can you hear the power chords? Can you hear the taunting lyrics? Can you hear the swaggering attitude? That was me, in the second stage of my management career and I imagine it was also a lot of other people, too.

We really begin to think of ourselves in this second phase of the manager's growth process as wearing kind of a metaphorical black leather jacket with chains. We kind of think of ourselves as perched up against a Harley Davidson in the company parking lot, looking cool in our biker gear.

It is very, very easy to become a Rebel when you realize that enthusiasm alone is not going to get the job done. And it even delivers results ...sometimes ... in the very short term. But over the long term (like, say, more than a month) it costs way too much and delivers way too little.

Being the Rebel means, almost by definition, that you start making certain mistakes as a manager. At the time, we may not realize our mistakes, but they are mistakes, and they are big ones. We start telling people what to do and making them do it our way. We start telling people who have been around for a while that they may resist you but that there's a new set of rules to play by – Rebel rules – and that resistance is futile. And at some point, when things aren't going quite the way we want them to, we get really, really angry at our staff – perhaps everybody at the same time.

And we turn them into little Rebels. And we wonder why our team doesn't perform the way it should.

By the way, you can be a quiet person and be just as Rebellious as a loud person – by using sarcasm, disapproval, or even silence to underscore this exact same message: *Things are different now, and if you don't do them my way, there is going to be trouble.* From the outside, somebody who does not know the organization very well might assume that a quiet person was conforming to everything that had been done before. But if we look at what is actually being put forward in staff meetings, and if we look at how this manager interacts over the long term with the direct reports and colleagues and senior people in his or her world, you realize that you're looking at somebody in this second, Rebellious stage of managerial development.

For some people, this Rebel stage of development lasts for a short period of time, and for other people, it lasts for a long period of time. Some people, unfortunately, never move past this second phase.

Point to ponder: **Spending too much time in the "Rebellion" phase is hazardous to your team's health – and to yours.**

Being a habitual Rebel manager carries a certain toll, emotionally and physically. You may find that your stomach is in knots a lot. You may feel tension in your shoulders. You may find yourself being snippy on a regular basis when you make it home at the end of the day. You may find yourself getting aggravated in traffic in a way that you never did before. If you notice any of those symptoms, beware. You are in the second, and potentially the most dangerous, phase of your development as a manager: the Rebel stage. You are fighting the rules, you are rebelling against precedent and experience, and you are operating on the assumption that the problem, if there is one, is always Out There, and not connected to you or your choices. And (here's the kicker), you are doing all this in a way that is probably causing severe physical and emotional stress to you, and the members of your team.

Does this ring any bells at all? Forget about your own experience for a moment. As you do today's assignment, think about *other* managers you have seen and/or worked for who seem to be in this second, rebellious, phase of their managerial career.

Pull out your notebook!

In your notebook, write the names of three managers you can remember encountering who seemed to be stuck in a "Rebel" stage of development.

What specific incidents, comments, or decisions suggest to you that these people were operating on the assumption that the problem, if there was one, was always Out There, and not connected to them or their choices as a manager? (Here's a big hint: Rebels are focused on the question, "Whose fault is this?")

⇥ ⇤

Bragging Rights!

Do not move on to Day 10 today,
or any other day in this book.

Complete the short written assignment (above)
in your notebook before you continue.

The Managerial Growth Cycle – *Flourishing*

E ntry to the third, and most critical, phase of managerial development must be preceded by a *decision point*.

You – not your boss, not your direct reports, not the crazy lady who's writing this book, but *you* have to decide that the costs of being a Rebel are simply too high ... and *you* have to make a strategic choice.

You have to decide to play the game.

And it *is* a game. It's *just* a game.

It's like what probably happened to you (and *definitely* happened to me) in high school. For me, there came a point in my rather rebellious high school career when my mom sat me down and said, "Look. This whole high school thing is just a game. Like any good game, it has rules. Just follow the rules and see what happens. Do your homework, study for your tests, make an effort ... and you'll still be yourself at the end of the day. You'll just be someone who knows how to play the game a little bit better than some other people do."

She was right, and she was also prefiguring my decision to move out of the Rebellion phase and into the Flourishing phase of my managerial career. That, too, was a matter of learning how to play a game. It was a question of knowing how to play by the rules in a way that *didn't* mean I had less integrity or personal authenticity than I had before. *All it meant was that I knew more about how people actually got things accomplished within my organization.*

Point to ponder: It's a game.
It's *just* a game. Play it well!

Play the game well, if you're going to play it! Play it in such a way that your team members aren't sitting around scratching their heads, wondering what the rules are.

The next time you're tempted to ask the habitual question of the Rebel manager ("Whose fault is this?"), challenge yourself instead to ask one or more of the following questions that managers in the Flourishing phase ask:

- What did I do to create this situation?
- What are the real-world benefits and costs of this situation?
- What resources are at my disposal to deal with this situation?
- What's my short-term objective in dealing with this situation?
- What's my long-term objective?

- What would a strong manager do in this situation? (If you have a particular manager you're using as a personal role model, feel free to use that person's example as a guide in answering this question.)
- What can I as a manager do right now to change this situation for the better?
- What can I do that will help us feel more connected as a team?
- What can I do that will improve communication?
- What can I do that will help us engage with one another?
- What can I do with the resources I have now to bring this team together?
- What "internal mantra" can I popularize for this team that will win buy-in, and help us all focus on the right stuff?

Not everyone moves out of the second phase of the managerial career into the third phase, but those who do are glad that they made the shift.

There are managers who finally do get tired of the costs

associated with the "them against me" way of looking at the world. They move into a third phase that I call Flourishing.

This Flourishing can only take place when people choose to take different steps and *grow* in ways that elude managers who still consider themselves Rebels. This is where you say, "Alright, maybe I need to look at me a little bit. I don't want to stay where I was so I need to learn a new way of being so that I can survive in this environment and do a little bit more than survive – and do a little bit more than survive. I want to do well here, so I am going to start trying some new ways of working with people."

The third phase of managerial development only happens when the manager in question makes a conscious choice to change the rebellious behaviors and adopt a new way of looking at managing people. The managers who Flourish want to thrive ... not just survive.

Rebels frequently focus on this notion of "survival." And, often that is all that they do: survive. The people who are at the third level have a very different goal. They want to do well. They want to shine. They want to expand their influence and their rewards... so they *change* what they are doing and they start by looking at themselves.

For me, the third phase of development began when I started asking myself a fateful question: "What do I need to do to flourish in this environment?" And, when I started asking that question, I started focusing on what kind of changes I needed to make *on my side* in order to excel. I became willing to take steps that would change my relationships with my team members from "You're either with me or you're against me" to something more positive and constructive.

Yes, that even applied to people who, through my Rebel phase, I had considered to be pains in the posterior. When I was in the flourishing phase, I was relating to them in a way that allowed me to see the value that even these difficult people brought to the table. Not only that: I found new ways to realize how I, as a person and a manager, could grow as a result of finding new potential in those "difficult" team members.

At this third phase, when I ran into someone who, in my earlier, Rebel phase, I would have simply written off as being harsh or difficult or uncooperative, I asked a different question and received a different insight on the experience. I start asking myself things like, "What can I learn from my interaction with this person?" "What has that person done to teach me something new about dealing with people effectively?" "What can I learn from this interaction that will make me a better manager?" "What new approach can I take in terms of communication, delegation, or emphasis that will help this person to accomplish something important even though his or her style doesn't match well with mine?"

In the third, Flourishing phase, the "problem employee" becomes less of an enemy and more of a resource waiting to be deployed.

Being in the flourishing state in your career as a manager is not at all unlike being a partner in a successful, long-term marriage. When you talk to people about long-term marriages that have succeeded over time and you ask them about the stages of their relationship, you always find that there is a period in the relationship where there was once an adversarial approach to some question or challenge – but the partners somehow found a way to step back, move away from a "me against you" mindset, and *learn* from their partners. They started thinking about what lesson *about the relationship* could be gained from the situation. This turning point is a common feature in every long-term relationship I have ever studied, and I think you may conclude this is a major factor for success in the long-term marriages you have encountered in your life.

A very similar mental shift takes place when we as managers learn, not on an intellectual level, but in the "gut," to step away from the Rebel mindset and begin learning from the people on our staff. Just as in a marriage, there is damage to the relationship if we throw on our leather jacket and win arguments by saying (or implying) things like "If you don't like it you can leave." Such messages are often signs of a relationship – and a team – in crisis.

In the Flourishing model, a manager makes the assumption that there is a commitment to working things out. The manager doesn't delude himself or herself into believing that it is feasible, or even possible, to change the employee. Instead, the manager makes a commitment to *change himself or herself*, and see the relationship from a different point of view.

So. Suppose I'm a Flourishing manager. What do I do about the "problem employee" who's currently driving me crazy?

Well, if I do not decide to get rid of this person, I personally have the responsibility to manage my communications in such a way that this relationship supports me as a manager. I can get there by any number of roads – including holding weekly coaching meetings, sharing the Starter Form strategy, and developing a "bragging rights" performance evaluation program that is uniquely suited to this person's working style. (You're going to read about how to put that program together a little later in this book.)

Ultimately, though, my outcome has to be to change *my* behavior in a way that makes this relationship supportive for me as a manager. If that does not happen, I must move forward with the difficult but necessary task of removing the person from the team. Notice that I should only do this *after* I have exhausted all the possible opportunities, within the limits of my resources, to improve the relationship and get the outcome I need. Notice that, even here, the status of the relationship is my responsibility.

Bragging Rights!

Nobody else is responsible for my relationship with this "problem employee." I accept that this relationship is my responsibility, and that it has a number of possible outcomes, including a parting of the ways.

When I choose to Flourish, I don't get distracted with the question of "how you relate to me." *How I relate to you* is what I can affect. That's what I focus on.

This is how managers who thrive, not just survive, do it. They ask better questions and take personal responsibility for how they relate to the people on their team.

Once you have experienced life in the Flourishing phase, my guess is that you'll want to stay there. You might stick your toe back into the Rebel mode from time to time, but you will always want to go back to that Flourishing level. You may fall back temporarily, but once you see the results, the passion, and the commitment that a commitment to Flourishing delivers in your team, and once you realize how satisfying it is to you as a person, you will always want to get back (as it were) to where you once belonged.

Pull out your notebook!

In your notebook, write down the names of three managers you have either worked for or come in contact with who made a successful transition from the Rebel phase of managerial development to the Flourishing phase of managerial development.

What evidence do you have that the change took place?

Do not move on to Day 11 today,
or any other day in this book.

Complete the short written assignment (above)
in your notebook before you continue.

*The Managerial Growth Cycle – **The Visionary***

S o what happens after the Flourishing phase if you're a manager? Is there anywhere to go after that?

As it happens, there is. The fourth phase is where you become a Visionary.

Here, you are on a mission. It's almost a religious calling. You are on a journey that is larger than your team's cumulative job description.

Visionaries don't ask themselves, "How am I going to hit quota?" They ask themselves, "How are we going to make a difference – how are we going to change people's lives?"

So in this fourth phase, the Visionary phase, we're talking not just about our team and its outcomes, but our ability to transform the lives of the team and everyone it touches! That's what you want to be moving toward.

Visionaries don't just get a product out the door. They don't just meet deadlines. These managers create experiences that bring people together, or create powerful memories, or help people provide for their families. Whatever *ultimate* benefit you could attach to a bolt, or an insurance policy, or a piece of software, or a training program, you can bet that the manager that is in this fourth, or Visionary phase of his or her career will focus on that positive outcome, and be energized by it.

The Visionary brings the game to a higher level. As a Visionary, you adopt a set of beliefs, values, and habits that set you apart from just about everyone else in the organization. You look at your company's people, products, and services and you don't see "insurance" or "bolts" –

you see a large scale process that improves the lives of *everyone who could conceivably be touched by that process.* That means customers, your team members, your company's stockholders – everybody. And you stay awake at night trying to find ways to make sure that that process delivers a positive outcome to *everyone* who connects with it.

Not every manager is cut out to be a full-fledged Visionary. Many good managers reach the Flourishing stage and stay there, and lead productive and satisfying careers. But you can at least move toward *becoming* a Visionary ... if you take an abiding interest in *understanding how what you as a manager do impacts the people who work for you.* If you do that, you'll want to know ...

- How can you deliver improvements in the lives and outlooks of the people who are your direct reports?
- How can your communication affect, in a profoundly positive way, the lives of the people who work for you? (Not just on the job, but off the job as well.)

- How does your communication with your team members affect the way they look at work? At life? At their family relationships?

If you routinely ask these kinds of questions about yourself, your team, and your communication patterns, you will be moving toward the Visionary phase of your career as a manager. If those kinds of questions energize you, excite you, give you a positive outlook on your own world, then you will know for sure that you have not stopped cold in your career.

And, if by some chance you *have* hit a snag, and perhaps overlooked opportunities to move from the Rebel phase to the Flourishing phase, or from the Flourishing phase to the Visionary phase, then my question for you is a simple one.

How much is your choice to not pursue a course of growth costing you, your team, and your company?

Now here's the payoff for moving toward the Visionary phase: A former "problem" employee approaches you in private and says, "I'm so glad you confronted me a few months back about my habit of talking myself down – other people had tried to challenge me on that for years, but the way you communicated the message to me, and the fact that it was *you* that did it, has really helped me to change my life. And a few weeks ago I met this amazing woman – and I know for a fact I would never have met this woman if it hadn't been for you. Thank you so much!"

Isn't that kind of an exchange worth a little extra effort on your part? (If you even thought about answering "Yes," you have the makings of a Visionary.)

Pull out your notebook!

Identify at least one person you have met who qualifies as a Visionary.

Write a description of that person in your notebook.

Did that person change your life for the better? If so, how?

Bragging Rights!

*Do not move on to Day 12 today,
or any other day in this book.*

*Complete the short written assignment (above)
in your notebook before you continue.*

Your Return On Investment

oing a better job of communicating with your employees will help them ... but it will also help *you* move forward through the four phases of your development as a manager.
That's your return on investment.

Look at the four phases of growth one more time:

- Enthusiasm

- Rebellion
- Flourishing
- Visionary

The more quickly and effectively you transform through these four phases (and, especially, the quicker you get out of Rebellion), the easier it will be for you to build alliances and secure the resources you need. To put a single, overused, but generally accurate word on this payoff, the more progress toward the Visionary stage you make, the more effective you will become as a *leader*.

An interesting thing happens as you become an effective leader: A kind of "centrifugal force" kicks in, and you find yourself with allies and tools that you didn't even ask for, but that turn out to be exactly what you and your team need to hit your goals. This may sound strange or even borderline-supernatural, but I've seen it happen too many times to believe that it isn't reality.

Point to ponder: **Managers who move toward the Visionary phase attract the people, opportunities, relationships, and resources they need to, often (seemingly) with little or no effort!**

Here's another interesting thing I've noticed about Visionary managers: They're almost always involved in some kind of charitable activity. They're the ones who are going on a walk for hunger and asking if people want to sponsor them. Now, they don't guilt-trip team members or anyone else into going on the walk with them ... but they do make a personal effort to make a difference in the lives of people outside their immediate sphere, and they usually do try to find ways to give the people they know in the workplace the opportunity to make some kind of relatively painless contribution to that effort. (Like sponsoring them on the walk.) Visionaries are *energized* by this kind of activity.

Something else you should know about managers who

make this journey: most of them develop an excellent sense of humor, and encourage their team members to laugh. That's more important than one might at first think. Teams with a corporate culture that allows people to laugh spontaneously during planning meetings, and whose most senior person models the behavior of laughing spontaneously during planning meetings, tend to achieve more than teams where laughter is seen as inappropriate.

Barking and screaming and yelling about mistakes kills spontaneity and laughter and camaraderie; this kind of management is essentially Rebel behavior. "You are going to do it my way and like it!" That's not the kind of message that loosens people up. Instead, it generally delivers strained silence and the kind of behind-the-scenes griping that turns employees into Rebels! People who move toward Visionary take a different approach. By encouraging the truth-telling and emotional openness that leads to constructive laughter, they build cohesion among teams.

When you are a Visionary, your people will be more motivated, more committed, and more inspired to do the very best job they possibly can. They will also be getting a lot more out of the job. And they will be getting more out of life. (By the way: So will you!)

You will know that you have reached the Visionary phase of your career when something like the following happens. You will have just wrapped up a team meeting, and one of your direct reports will approach you one-on-one and say: "I've got to tell you, when we were having that team meeting and you were talking about setting meaning-ful goals for ourselves, it hit me in a really powerful way and it made a big difference to me. In fact, that actually seemed relevant to my family, and I wanted you to know that I will be sharing what you said at home tonight. That was great stuff. Thank you very much."

When you hear something like that at the end of one of your team meetings, you will know you are pointed in the right direction. On the other hand, if you *never* hear any-thing like that, there is a good chance that you are not get-ting the most out of your team ... or yourself as a manager.

To make the journey toward becoming a true Vision-ary manager, I think you must look with attention, com-mitment, and passion at each of your team members, and identify what his or her strong suit, or "sweet spot" actually is. **You cannot be a Visionary and not care deeply about what each unique member of your team has to offer**. If you only have a vague sense of what each individual person on your team is uniquely capable of contributing to the process of working for you, there's still some work to do.

In the following chapters, I am going to share with you four very different "road maps" that will help you make a journey toward a particular kind of person who is almost certainly already on your team. Each of these destinations corresponds with a particular **working style**.

In other words: there are four primary working styles you should understand, and each of the four is probably relevant to someone who reports to you right now. I know people tend to be skeptical when they see yet another breakdown of "personality styles" in the workplace, I was skeptical as well when I first encountered these models. But they are startlingly, even frighteningly, accurate predictors of four distinct, and vitally important, ways of approaching work as part of a team. My prediction is that, as you read through them, you will find that they do indeed match up with colleagues you already know well, or even with your-self. The question is...**how well do the four working styles match up with the people whose talents you may not yet know quite as well?** (Your own direct reports, say.)

In order to have an effective and intelligent perfor-mance evaluation session with your direct report, you have to know what he or she does well and enjoys doing. If you constantly lecture and complain about things that the per-son does not and cannot do well, then you are going to have problems during the personnel evaluation.

If, on the other hand, you use the information you'll find in Days 12 through 19 to get clarity on what each of your team members *does* do well, what he or she *could* be contributing, and what else you *could* be measuring that you're not measuring right now, then you will be in a much better position to improve both the quality of the evalua-tion meeting and the person's commitment to your depart-ment. And once you take *that* kind of interest in the people who report to you, you will in fact be moving toward Vi-sionary status as a manager.

In my research on teams, I was exposed to the outstand-

ing research of Allen Fahden and Marie West, authors of
<u>How to End Hare-Turtle Wars and Create Amazing Results Doing What You Love</u>. Their work was highlighted by
Mark Victor Hansen and Robert Allen in their chapter on
"Dream Teams" in the New York Times bestseller <u>The One
Minute Millionaire</u>. The following process and descriptors
are based on their wonderful writings combined with my
research, experience, and insights.

It's sad but true. Most of us are Rebel managers, and
most Rebel managers have no idea what their team members should really be doing. We have a much better sense
of what we *don't* want people to do. We spend most of our
time focusing on who is responsible for mistakes, omissions,
or even a failure to read our minds. When we are in Rebel
mode, we focus obsessively on who is to blame. And by doing that, we foster an environment in which the primary job
skill is "covering your anatomy."

That was *me*, in my Rebel mode. Does this ring any
bells for *you*?

In the days that follow, you will identify which of your
team's *intrinsic* assets you, as a manager, should be track-

ing, reinforcing, and using to get good work done. Once you know what that good stuff is – I call this good stuff the employee's "working style" or "sweet spot" – you can ask the person who reports to you to help you monitor each and every contribution he or she makes in that area. You can ask the employee to assume "bragging rights" for everything that happens in that special area that corresponds to his or her *intrinsic* way of approaching the world of work.

And guess what? People love keeping track of stuff that they know they're good at doing.

Pull out your notebook!

Where are you in your managerial journey right now? Enthusiastic? Rebellious? Flourishing? Visionary?

Write at least five sentences identifying your current dominant style, and giving examples to support your case.

Bragging Rights!

✢ ✢

Do not move on to Day 13 today,
or any other day in this book.

Complete the short written assignment (above)
in your notebook before you continue.

Bragging Rights For The Salesperson

*Y*our employee, Joe, could have a SALESPERSON working style.

Don't think of the SALESPERSON as somebody who earns a commission to sell products and services. For our purposes, a SALESPERSON is someone whose talent and ability is being able to select ideas that could easily be "sold" to other people. Most people with a SALESPERSON working style do not have the responsibility of meeting a sales quota. Plenty of people who sell for a living do not have the SALESPERSON working style.

I don't care if your team consists of nurses or nuclear physicists: The odds are very good that somebody in your group has this talent. This person knows what will "fly" and what won't. If Joe is your SALESPERSON, he knows a good idea when he hears one, and he gets very excited. Joe is the person who, when you're in the middle of a brainstorming session, suddenly says, "This is the idea that's going to work – this one, right here." Joe is also the one who inevitably has a good, solid sense of which is the best one to put forward as the "public face" of the project you're working on.

Those of us who don't necessarily have this skill may sometimes be tempted to conclude that Joe's ability to pick the idea that "will fly" is a simplistic, superficial, or inconsequential contribution to the discussion. Nothing could be further from the truth. In any organization, being able to gauge the reaction of outside groups—potential customers, stockholders, regulatory officials, whoever—is an essential skill, and failing to take advantage of that skill is the kind of thing that drives the SALESPERSON nuts. (It can also drive the project itself into the ground.)

Suppose you have a "brainstorming" meeting with your team. You want people to get creative and go a little crazy. You want to walk away with a bunch of ideas. Once you've gone through that process, what if you dismissed the group and, during a one-on-one meeting, showed that list of ideas to Joe, your SALESPERSON?

If he's a SALESPERSON, Joe will be able to identify for you exactly which of those 30 ideas will or will not work from the point of view of your internal or external customers. He'll know which ones people would likely ignore or shoot down. He also knows which ones have the strongest likelihood of being accepted. Joe will be able to pick out which idea could capture somebody else's imagination and encourage further interest and buy-in. SALESPEOPLE have a talent within them to see immediately that which excites them, and which is likely to excite other people. SALESPEOPLE know which ideas inspire positive emotions. That's a very important talent. And if somebody on your staff—Joe, say—possesses it, **you should know that**

and grant Joe bragging rights over achievements in the area of spotting the idea an internal or external customer will like.

The SALESPERSON is likely to be good at the following tasks:

- Choosing a name or theme for a party that everyone would want to attend.
- Critiquing a headline in the company newsletter, or tweaking it so that it becomes much more interesting.
- Picking the right project name.
- Selecting the right conversational "hook" for a discussion about a product, service, or program.

Here's the challenge: Sometimes, your SALESPERSON may spend all day doing stuff that has nothing whatsoever to do with picking the right idea, the idea that other people will get excited about.

If that's the case, and Joe is currently answering phones for us at the reception desk, we are nevertheless going to find a way to put his talents to use.

Think of a SALESPERSON on your team. Have you got someone in mind?

Now come up with a (formal or informal) list of ideas for him or her to critique. Give this employee the chance to share his or her opinion about which of the ideas is best, and why the idea is likely to appeal to people outside his or her immediate workgroup.

Point to ponder: **If you are really dealing with a SALESPERSON, you will notice that the person responds quickly and with positive emotion when you ask for help in identifying the best ideas in a given area. The SALESPERSON will soon start giving you feedback you can use.**

If you wish, you can do a test by throwing a few ideas at Joe during a one-on-one conversation, and then asking for insights about which seems the most appealing. See what happens. If the employee quickly spots the best ideas, and separates out the rest, giving persuasive reasons why they would not appeal to the audience you're trying to reach, you may rest assured that you have hooked up someone whose primary working style is that of the SALESPERSON.

That's the pattern with this working style. Someone mentions a new approach to doing something, and the SALESPERSON practically jumps out of the chair and says, "That's it! That's the one! I could take that and show it to such-and-such a person and he'd love it!"

You should be preceding your individual employee evaluation meetings with this person by asking him or her to a) keep track of the "hottest" ideas or "sound bites" in areas X, Y, and Z over the next few weeks ... and b) submit this list to you privately at your next one-on-one meeting.

If you have identified the SALESPERSON correctly, you will receive no push-back or resistance whatsoever when you suggest this.

Joe will eagerly track, and quietly forward to you, the "cream of the crop" of the ideas he hears or helps to generate.

If the projects you're giving Joe don't currently involve this function, of determining which ideas are great and which ideas aren't, then you need to find a way to point this person toward that kind of activity for at least part of the day.

Pull out your notebook!

Based on what you learned today, identify at least one SALESPERSON on your team.

Write a short description of that person in your notebook.

Answer this question: What is that person doing right now that matches up with the SALESPERSON working style?

Answer this question: What COULD this person do on an upcoming project that would match up with the SALESPERSON working style?

Bragging Rights!

Do not move on to Day 14 today,
or any other day in this book.

Complete the short written assignment (above)
in your notebook before you continue.

Bragging Rights For The Artist

Your employee, Joe, could have an ARTIST working style.

Let's return to that hypothetical meeting from yesterday. Let's assume that the brainstorming piece has just happened, and that everybody is up on their feet, looking at the various ideas that have been thrown up on the white board. And let's say that instead of jumping out of his seat and saying, "Idea X is really a great idea. I know that idea could fly!" Joe turns to you and says something like this:

> "Yeah, that would work ... if you did such and such before you got started. I could see that. Of course, you'd need to do A, B, and C as you roll this out. And you'd have to pick the right location, and the right time of year, and you'd have such-and-such scheduling issues to sort out. But if you did all that..."

In this example, Joe is focusing not on which idea or "hook" he could "sell" to an internal or external customer, but on *what would have to happen* for the project to succeed; who would actually have to do what, and when, and with whom. What would the itinerary look like? Where would people actually go? What would they do when they got there?

If Joe quickly starts generating a list of logistical issues that *connect* to a given idea, you're looking at a different kind of working style. This is the ARTIST.

You know that time you walked over to Joe's cubicle, and you heard him on the phone trying to reschedule his child's orthodontist appointment? Or heard him reorganizing the schedule of the bowling league he's a member of? Or watched him trying to book a flight online for one of his monthly weekend getaways with his family?

Remember how irritated you got with Joe then? You didn't say anything at the time (or maybe you did), but it's a cinch that you had something like this internal monologue: *Doesn't he realize this is an office? What is he doing wasting our day on that personal stuff? Why does he show so little respect for this organization? Why doesn't he do personal things on personal time?*

Good news, bad news department. The good news is that you were right about Joe screwing up by doing all that stuff on company time. The bad news is that, if you choose to challenge him on that at his next performance evaluation, you'll win the battle but lose the war. What Joe was really doing when he was "wasting time" on all those extracurricular logistical sessions was sending you a message. Whether he realized it or not, Joe was shouting, "Hey – I'm

Bragging Rights!

an ARTIST! Give me something to plan! Let me set up the logistics for something! Let me put together some kind of sequence of events for some project! I'm *great* at putting together itineraries! I'm *great* at figuring what should happen first, second, third, and last! In fact, when I'm not here, that's what people *ask me to do all the time,* because I'm so darned good at it. I love planning ... and I wish I were doing more of it for you."

Are you *sure* you want the meeting with Joe, the ARTIST, to be about how he spends too much time on the phone, on the computer, and online coordinating things?

ARTISTS know what has to happen next in order for the project to actually get off the ground. And if somebody on your staff—Joe, say—possesses that talent, **you should know that and grant Joe bragging rights over planning achievements.**

The ARTIST is likely to be good at the following tasks:

- Figuring out what has to happen, in what order, if your team is moving from one location to another.
- Identifying the best way to get a company newslet-

98

ter out to the people who might read it.

- Giving you a good estimate of when something will be finished.

- Handling the setup and execution of a company event. Pick any important event your company stages; watch what your company's people actually do before, during, and after the event. I guarantee you that there will always be one person that your company's people run to *first* to answer an important question. Regardless of his or her job title, that person is an ARTIST.

Here's the challenge: Sometimes, your ARTIST may spend all day doing stuff that has nothing whatsoever to do with figuring out what should happen first, second, third, and last.

If that's the case, and Joe is currently doing something other than planning, we are nevertheless going to find a way to put his talents to use.

Think of an ARTIST on your team. Have you got someone in mind?

Now come up with some process for him or her to set up. It should involve other people. Give this employee the chance to share his or her opinion about what should happen first, second, third, and last on an upcoming project.

Point to ponder: **If you are dealing with an ARTIST, you will notice that the person responds quickly and with positive emotion when you ask for help in identifying what should happen first, second, third, and last. The ARTIST will soon start giving you a proposed sequence of events that you can really use.**

You should be preceding your individual employee evaluation meetings with this person by asking him or her to a) build some kind of proposed process or plan that involves at least two people (yes, the ARTIST can be one of them) ... and b) submit this plan to you privately at your next one-on-one meeting so you can discuss it together.

If you have identified the ARTIST correctly, you will

receive no push-back or resistance whatsoever when you suggest this.

Joe will eagerly track, and quietly forward to you, the very best plans and processes that he generates or helps to generate.

If the projects you're giving Joe don't currently involve this ARTISTIC function, then you need to find a way to point Joe toward that kind of activity for at least part of the day.

Pull out your notebook!

Based on what you learned today, identify at least one ARTIST on your team.

Write a short description of that person in your note-book.

Answer this question: What is that person doing right now that matches up with the ARTIST working style?

Answer this question: What COULD this person do

on an upcoming project that would match up with the ARTIST working style?

＋≫ ≪＋

Do not move on to Day 15 today,
or any other day in this book.

Complete the short written assignment (above)
in your notebook before you continue.

Bragging Rights For The Planner

*Y*our employee, Joe, could have a PLANNER working style.

Let's return to our hypothetical meeting. We've thrown out a whole bunch of ideas on the board, and everyone is looking at the ideas we've collected. This time, Joe doesn't jump out of his seat in excitement about one particular idea. Nor does he suggest a list of things that would need to happen for the idea to become a reality. No, with this version of Joe, we hear what sounds an awful lot like skepticism. We hear Joe share some variation on the comment, "That's not going to work, because ..."

This working style belongs to the PLANNER – sometimes known as the devil's advocate.

The PLANNER is frequently misunderstood. Some people hear Joe's skeptical reactions to ideas and conclude – wrongly – that he is an inherently cynical or negative team member. In fact, PLANNERS are entirely focused on a *positive* outcome for the team. They simply want to remove all the potential obstacles to that positive outcome. And they do this by means of a "troubleshooting" mindset.

PLANNERS may make great engineers, scientists, accountants, quality control professionals, or attorneys. They may *remind* you of people in these professions, which can be either a good thing or a bad thing, depending on the setting where they're expressing themselves.

These folks have a working style that allows them to spot potentially project-destroying crises before they happen. Far from being a negative influence on the team, they can, if plugged in at the right point of the process, save the entire undertaking from disaster. *But....* you, the manager, have to make sure that their efforts are pointed in the right direction.

The PLANNER is the one who looks at everything and says, "Have you thought about this? Or this? Or this?"

The PLANNER is the one who shows up for a meeting and says, "All right, I've looked everything over and ... and here are some of the issues we're going to need to think about to avoid (insert potentially catastrophic problem here)."

The PLANNER is the one who walks into the room with a big grin on her face and says, "Such-and-such may cause the system to crash... but I think I found a work-around."

At some point, the PLANNERS and the ARTISTS have to have a series of exchanges. The PLANNERS will spot a problem. The ARTISTS will say, "Oh, I see. Yeah, that is a problem. All right, we can do X, Y and Z to avoid that." At which point, the PLANNERS say, "Well, X would work, but Y doesn't make any sense because that solution leaves you open to (insert other potentially catastrophic problem here)." And the discussion goes on, usually quite productively.

Here's the thing to understand about PLANNERS: They're not really great at coming up with original ideas. But that doesn't mean that they are not creative. They're just creative in a different (and extremely important) direction. They keep disasters from happening. We like that, right?

We may be able to spot Joe for the PLANNER that he is if we catch him shooting down somebody else's idea. This is a classic activity for people with this working style. In fact, PLANNERS sometimes have major social problems around this issue, because the tendency is so strongly pronounced. They are really not trying to diminish or show disrespect to others – well not always – but if they see a technical problem or a potential disaster waiting to happen, they simply can't keep silent about it. That's why they sometimes look extremely uncomfortable when participating in "brainstorming sessions" where the ground rules forbid shooting down a bad idea. If you notice that one of your team members is extremely restless during a session like this "brainstorming," that's another very good signal that that person is a PLANNER.

PLANNERS are all about figuring out what could conceivably go wrong when the project hurtles into the real world. And if somebody on your staff—Joe, say -- possesses that talent, **you should know that and grant Joe bragging rights over spotting and preventing disasters.**

The PLANNER is likely to be good at the following tasks:

- Figuring out what systems won't work properly once your team tries to reboot the computer.
- Spotting typos in the company newsletter.
- Giving you a good estimate of what specific factors could keep the team from completing a project on time.
- Telling a potential customer what might possibly go wrong somewhere down the line if the customer should be so foolish as to actually buy something from your organization. (This is an endearing habit that has produced friction between sales managers and PLANNERS for some centuries now.)

Bragging Rights!

Here's the challenge: Sometimes, your PLANNER may spend all day doing stuff that has nothing whatsoever to do with spotting things that could conceivably go wrong.

If that's the case, and Joe is currently doing something other than identifying potential problems, we are nevertheless going to find a way to put his talents to use.

Think of a PLANNER on your team. Have you got someone in mind?

Great. Now here comes the easiest part of this book. There is no member of the team whose evaluation session is simpler to set up than the PLANNER.

Before your session with this person, simply say something along the following lines:

"Joe, I'm very concerned about the possibility of oversights and omissions and quality problems in the so and so area. Over the next couple of weeks, I'd like you to keep a private journal on places where you think we may run into problems that nobody else has seen. Could I ask you to jot those down and share them with me once a week?"

No one else on the team will respond as positively and enthusiastically to this request as the PLANNER.

Point to ponder: **If you are really dealing with a PLANNER, you will notice that the person responds quickly and with positive emotion when you ask for help in identifying potentially serious problems or oversights. The PLANNER will soon start giving you a long list of potentially project-shredding flaws. Keep that list private until you decide what action(s) you plan to take on it.**

If the projects you're giving Joe to work on don't currently involve this troubleshooting function, then you need to find a way to point Joe toward that kind of activity for at least part of the day.

Pull out your notebook!

Based on what you learned today, identify at least one PLANNER on your team.

Write a short description of that person in your notebook.

Answer this question: What is that person doing right now that matches up with the PLANNER working style?

Answer this question: What COULD this person do on an upcoming project that would match up with the PLANNER working style?

◈ ◈ ◈

*Do not move on to Day 16 today,
or any other day in this book.*

*Complete the short written assignment (above)
in your notebook before you continue.*

Bragging Rights For The Soldier

Your employee, Joe, could have a SOLDIER working style.

During that team meeting of ours, the SOLDIER is the person who just wants to get down to business and get started. If Joe is a SOLDIER, Joe says, "Give me the plan. Tell me what needs to be done. And I'll get it done."

These people have a single-minded focus. Their attitude is

pretty simple: "Get out of my way. Don't change the rules on me. Just let me do it." SOLDIERS don't really want to do the creative stuff. They don't want to do the fact checking. They don't want to do the trouble shooting. And they certainly don't want to be bothered with the "how" of the project. They just want to get started. They want to get into the batting cage and take the swings and make some stuff happen.

They don't want to be criticized, and they certainly don't want to be criticized for something they have been following instructions on. If there is a problem, anywhere along the line, it won't be because they didn't follow orders.

You can expect SOLDIERS to say things like, "But that's not what you told me to do," or, "I'm just doing what you said." If you see any of these behaviors or hear any of these comments from somebody on your team, you are very likely to be dealing with a SOLDIER.

It's quite likely that, during team meetings, the SOLDIER will be the quietest person in the room. You can expect the SALESPERSON to jump up and down with enthusiasm about a specific idea that he knows he, she, you or the team can pitch to someone outside of the group. You can expect the ARTIST to start a discussion about how the project would actually roll out and what resources would be needed to make it happen. You can expect the PLAN-NER to highlight potential flaws within the working plan proposed by the ARTIST. While all of this is happening, you can expect the SOLDIER to say little or nothing. In fact, they're often at a loss about how to make a contribution during team meetings. A classic managerial mistake is to criticize the SOLDIER for this, or take away brownie points for "not contributing to discussions."

Think twice, three times, or, if need be, a thousand times before you criticize the SOLDIER for being silent during team meetings. Once the plan is settled, you'll hear some variation on this from the person who has remained quiet through most of the proceedings up to this point: "So what do I do?" Those are the magic words! The SOLDIER is an essential person to have on your team. This is the person who gets in there and does stuff. Not only that, but most SOLDIERS are in heaven when they get to put together the to-do list and makes sure that everything on it gets done when it's supposed to get done. We like that, right?

SOLDIERS are all about completing the mission. They don't want to plan, fix or sell... they want to do. And if somebody on your staff—Joe, say – possesses that talent, **you should know that and grant Joe bragging rights so they can complete the mission of the team.**

The SOLDIER is likely to be good at the following tasks:

- Keeping the master checklist about anything.
- Putting printouts of the company newsletter in everybody's mailbox.
- Getting the warehouse cleaned out on or before the time they promised to have it cleaned out.
- Catching up a new team member (or anyone else) about what has happened up to this point on a project.
- Making sure you, the manager, have accurate updates about how much of the to-do list has been completed, how much hasn't, and how much time remains to complete it.

Here's the challenge: Sometimes, your SOLDIER may spend all day doing stuff that has nothing whatsoever to do with keeping the master to-do list up to date.

If that's the case, and Joe is currently doing something other than figuring out what's been done and what hasn't been done on some project on your list, we are still going to find a way to put his talents to use.

Think of a SOLDIER on your team. Have you got someone in mind?

In your pre-performance evaluation discussions with this person, you should ask him or her to keep track of which tasks in a given area have actually been done and which still remain to be done.

You should not ask this person for creative input. You should not ask this person to set up the plan or write the plan. You should not ask this person to troubleshoot the plan. Ask this person for help in keeping track of what's already been completed, what can't yet be crossed off the list, and how much time the team has to finish the job.

Point to ponder: **If you are dealing with a SOLDIER, you will notice that the person responds quickly and with positive emotion when assignments and tasks are given and he or she can just "do it" and get the job done.**

If the projects you're giving Joe to work on don't currently involve this to-do focus, then you need to find a way to point Joe toward that kind of activity for at least part of the day.

Pull out your notebook!

Based on what you learned today, identify at least one SOLDIER on your team.

Write a short description of that person in your notebook.

Answer this question: What is that person doing right now that matches up with the SOLDIER'S working style?

Answer this question: What COULD this person do on an upcoming project that would match up with the SOLDIER'S working style?

↦ ↤

Do not move on to Day 17 today,
or any other day in this book.

Complete the short written assignment (above)
in your notebook before you continue.

DAY 17:

Reality Check

B ased on the work you've done over the last few days, have you come up with some new approaches to the question of *whose issue it really is* when you tell team members to do something ... and they don't do it to your satisfaction?

It's time for a reality check. You as a manager have the critical responsibility of finding out which working style each and every one of your team members fall into. You as a manager have the critical responsibility of making sure that some, most, or all (your choice) of the assignments you hand out to your people fall within their working style "strike zone."

Sure, there are other reasons a member of your team might not complete a task on time, might not perform up to the quality level you expect, or might not have the same agenda you do. Some of those reasons do in fact lie outside of your control. But the most important possible reason for these kinds of problems – the reason I'm going to challenge you to focus on today – is the reason you *do* have control over. Namely: the number of things you've asked this person to do that *actually match up with his or her working style*.

Suppose you still aren't certain whether a given team member is a SALESPERSON, an ARTIST, a PLANNER, or a SOLDIER? The very best way to find out is to ask the person "What do people ask them to help them with during his or her *non-work* hours." And that's what I want you to do today.

It's surprisingly easy to "miscast" people, because they sometimes create workplace identities that mask or redirect their true skill sets. If you focus on what the person does *after* work, however, you'll be on the right track.

Suppose you find out that, in her spare time, one of your team members coordinates a weekly square dancing club – setting up schedules, identifying locales, coming up with new plans for club events based on ongoing discussions with each member of the club. *That person has the primary working style of the ARTIST, even if you have come to think of her as a SALESPERSON.*

TITLE	DEFINED ROLE
SALESPERSON	The SALESPERSON recognizes ideas and new directions in their early stages and develops the means to promote or advance them.
ARTIST	The ARTIST generates the concepts and ideas. They like to reframe the problem and look for solutions that may be unusual, unique and/or outside the boundaries of traditional thought. They enjoy creating the picture of the project, tasks, to do's, time frame, etc.
PLANNER	The PLANNER challenges concepts under discussion. Believing that consequences matter, the PLANNER will want to plan how new endeavors are implemented and prepare for surprises.
SOLDIER	The SOLDIER, more interested in protecting the system than being in the meeting, follows up on team objectives and implements ideas and solutions.

Bragging Rights!

Point to ponder: **If you learn who to put in the right spot, grant bragging rights, and reward them accordingly, you will grow as a manager ... and find, not too very long from now, that you have a superstar team on your hands.**

Pull out your notebook!

Today, talk informally with each of your team members. Your goal is to find out something about what each and every person on your team does on his or her private time.

Write what you learn about each person in your notebook.

Does what you learn support or contradict what you thought was true about the person's primary working style? Write down your answer to this question.

AND FINALLY, ANSWER THIS AT THE END OF

TODAY: Based on what you learned as the result of your discussions with your team members today, what is your best guess as to each team member's DOMINANT working style, and also each team member's SECONDARY or "backup" style? Who matches up with you best? Who are you going to have to build some bridges to connect with, simply based on the fact that you have sharply differing working styles?

⇥ ⇤

Do not move on to Day 18 today,
or any other day in this book.

Complete the short written assignment (above)
in your notebook before you continue.

The Perfect Process

Assume that you have one of each of the four working styles on your team:

SALESPERSON

ARTIST

PLANNER

SOLDIER

What would the ideal working process look like for a typical project?

I know. There's no such thing as a typical project. Here's my answer anyway.

STEP ONE: Imagine that you have a team meeting where people brainstorm for fifteen minutes about the very best ways to do the project or ideas connected to it. Ground rules: "Anything goes. Avoid criticizing or troubleshooting any idea, but if you absolutely must, you must. Once. We each get one chance, and only one chance, to say, 'That won't work.'" (If you try to *forbid* criticism outright, you'll alienate the PLANNER. If you try to run the meeting for longer than fifteen minutes, you'll alienate the SOLDIER.)

STEP TWO: Commit all the ideas to paper. After the meeting, give the sheet to the SALESPERSON. Either review the ideas with the SALESPERSON or let the SALESPERSON review them on his or her own. Either way, the process should be to isolate the very best ideas, initiatives, or headlines. Perhaps you started with forty ideas; by the end of Step Two, you should have whittled that down to, say, four.

STEP THREE: The SALESPERSON commits all of that "cream of the crop" information to flipchart sheets, leaving plenty of room for other people to add their own ideas beneath each "winning" idea. Post each big sheet on a wall in the meeting room. These are all solid ideas that we absolutely, positively can sell to our external customers, whether that is the janitor down the hall, whose workspace we are going to redesign, or the CEO of a company that we are trying to sell to.

STEP FOUR: Lead a team meeting. Write all over the four sheets on the wall. Work together to choose one of the four on the wall. This is going to become "the project." Now everyone in the team leaves the room . . . except for you and the ARTIST(S).

STEP FIVE: Lead a discussion with the ARTIST(S) whose topic is: "How do we do this?" In a collaborative discussion, build up a first draft of the plan, including a prioritized list of the things that need to be done. Post the list on the wall.

STEP SIX: Call the PLANNER back into the room for a one-on-one meeting. Say, "We need your help." Now this person, who may have been penalized for being "negative," and who may have been ostracized for being a "whiner," who may have never felt acknowledged within a team environment, *finally has the chance to shine.* This PLANNER will come in for fifteen or twenty minutes and work with you to isolate all the potential trouble points with the plan. He or she should create a written list and post it on the wall.

STEP SEVEN: While the PLANNER is still in the room, call the ARTIST back into the room and go over all the items on the PLANNER'S "could-go-wrong" list. ARTISTS tend to see solutions; PLANNERS tend to see potential problems. The two are likely to clash. Realize this, and strategize ways to move forward or work around each of the items on the list. Congratulations! Your PLANNER has just been validated! You and the ARTIST have taken the list seriously enough to figure out exactly how the potential problems could affect the plan and have developed action steps to resolve the issue.

At this point, you can expect to see something truly remarkable happen: the PLANNER will actually buy into the project. Hard to believe, I know, but once you have given this person this kind of validation of his or her role, you can expect to hear things like this "That's okay – you've dealt with my issues. I can get behind this."

STEP EIGHT: Call everybody back into the room. Review all the work that's been done up to this point, and distribute action items onto specific peoples' to do lists. Every action item should have someone who accepts ownership of it. Sometimes the SOLDIER will volunteer to take on the vast majority of these action items. Whether that happens or not, appoint the SOLDIER to help you keep track of exactly what has gotten done, what has not, and when the various items are supposed to be finished. (More than anyone else on the team, the SOLDIER really, really minds missing your deadlines.)

STEP NINE: Set a date and time for a status report meeting with the entire team.

STEP TEN: Hold that meeting. (Blowing it off, or postponing it without a really good reason, will demotivate the entire team, and drive certain team members, notably the SOLDER, up a wall.)

Expect all of your team members to take this process

very seriously. There should be a high level of personal accountability throughout this process; everybody will buy into it, because *no one is being told to do anything that's outside of their working style.*

Believe it! Your team will be motivated to perform like the champions that they are in this meeting. Why? Because you will have successfully identified their "sweet spot," you've challenged them to make something happen by using that God-given talent and capacity of theirs in a high-visibility way.

STEP	ACTION	TASK	WHO	STRENGTH
1	Streaming	All brainstorm, capture ideas, no negatives	ALL	
2	Promoting	SALESPERSON chooses highest priority idea(s)	SALESPERSON	Spontaneous/ Practical
3	Editing	PLANNER & SOLDIER identify possible obstacles to success	PLANNER & SOLDIER	Methodical/ Practical
4	Igniting	ARTIST ignites new ideas to overcome obstacles	ARTISTS	Conceptual/ Spontaneous
5	Editing	PLANNER & SOLDIER identify possible obstacles to success	PLANNER & SOLDIER	Conceptual/ Methodical & Methodical/ Practical
6	Doing	All plan launch for fast SOLDIER implementation	All Then SOLDIER	ALL plus Methodical/ Practical

Pull out your notebook!

Identify a specific upcoming project you could execute by means of the ten-step process described in this chapter. Describe the goal of the project in detail.

━╪━ ━╪━

*Do not move on to Day 19 today,
or any other day in this book.*

*Complete the short written assignment (above)
in your notebook before you continue.*

DAY 19:

Common Challenges

The most common mistake that managers make when it comes to dealing with the four different working styles is not to know that they exist.

You might never ask the receptionist, "Sally, how do you think we should be planning to execute the move from this building to the new facility?" But if Sally is the only ARTIST on your work team, you should be asking her that question.

Bragging Rights!

You might never think that the copywriter on your team might be a superior PLANNER. But if Jim is the only effective troubleshooter you have access to on your staff, you should be eliciting his thoughts on what might go wrong with the project. That "irritating" habit he has of penciling corrections on to company memos while he thinks no one is looking... What is that really telling you? If you spot this behavior, you might want to think about asking Jim what could conceivably go wrong when the company moves your team from one facility to another.

The customer service representative who handles incoming calls for your group might not instantly strike you as being a SALESPERSON. You might assume that because the person possesses a fair amount of product knowledge, you're looking at someone who has expertise in troubleshooting problems. But if you overhear Jill brainstorming about different ways to create a "buzz" for the company party by changing its stated theme from Hawaiian to Retro '60s, it is a pretty good bet you have a SALESPERSON on your hands. This is a person you should be asking, "Jill, which of these ideas do you think works best as a headline for an email message about the upcoming move to the new facility?"

If Bill, your senior sales professional, seems to you to be a "people person" simply by virtue of his job description, you should check your assumptions. Is he really a "big idea" guy, the sort of person who loves to brainstorm and share new thoughts and plans with others? Or is he instead the kind of sales professional who succeeds by taking advantage of a powerful determination to get things done? If you notice Bill, on his lunch hour, speaking on his cell phone to his wife, and reviewing all the things on the to do list that have not yet been completed during the renovation of his home, you should stop and ask yourself whether Bill, the SALES-PERSON, might actually be a SOLDIER, regardless of his formal job description. This might just be the person you would want to put in charge of keeping track of what has actually been completed, and what has yet to be done, on the master to do list you work out with the team for making a successful transition to your team's new work space.

Another common mistake that we may make as managers is to look for reasons to criticize a behavior that is intrinsic to someone's working style.

For instance, it is very easy for managers to dismiss the PLANNER as a "whiner" or as someone who refuses to "adopt a positive attitude." If you know someone on your team who seems to fit this description, step back and ask yourself whether he or she might benefit your next project by identifying potential catastrophic problems.

Similarly, it is easy to make major mistakes in assessing the skills of the ARTIST. This individual may be criticized for having "no follow-through." We may say of an underutilized or misplaced ARTIST, "She talks all day long, but she never actually does anything." Or: "He always seems to finish things at the last minute, or not to finish them at all." If this statement seems to apply to someone on your team, step back and ask yourself whether you may actually have an asset you're not utilizing fully – this person's ability to visualize exactly how a project should unfold. Another big mistake we make when dealing with this person is quizzing them about all the things that could possibly go wrong with an initiative, and then jumping all over them if they overlook one. Remember, ARTISTS are essentially optimistic. For this kind of analysis, you should be talking to the PLANNER.

I've met managers who made the mistake of giving the SALESPERSON lots of detail work to keep track of. *This is not their strong suit.* Remember, these are "big idea" people, and asking them to proofread a report or troubleshoot a piece of computer software may not be the best use of their time. If someone on your staff appears to "drop the ball" and overlook critical, but small, details, do a double-check and ask this person to do a quick critique on ten possible ideas for new initiatives. See which two or three the person selects. If the person picks the two or three strongest ideas, or, even better, comes up with a brand new idea that no one had considered before, you may well have a SALESPERSON waiting to make a contribution to your team.

Perhaps the saddest and most frustrating mistake managers make has to do with the SOLDIER. Sometimes, we will look at the experience or work history of a team member, and assume that he or she knows how to communicate persuasively and in a compelling way about an idea that *seems* to be connected to work they have done in the past. When this request of ours falls flat, we may conclude that the person "lacks initiative" or "cannot think on his feet."

Bragging Rights!

For instance: Suppose you were to ask a SOLDIER with experience in the field of accounting to pick the very best marketing slogan for an ad campaign designed to appeal to accountants. I realize it might be tempting to assume that this person's five years of accounting experience make him an expert analyzer of direct mail headlines, but this is *almost certainly not true*. Spotting the right headline is the SALESPERSON'S job. If we force SOLDIERS to make this kind of choice, they will usually become restless, drum their fingers on the table, and seem quite uncomfortable. It is almost as if they are saying, "You mean if I pick one of these headlines, the meeting will be over and I can go back to my job?" It's not terribly surprising that when we ask SOLDIERS to do things that do not play to their "sweet spot," they disengage from the process and do not deliver the results we want. (Many SOLDIERS are criticized for "refusing to contribute to team meetings." Actually, they *live* to contribute ... they just have a hard time hiding their boredom with things that don't have anything to do with knocking things off a to-do list in a timely manner.)

In all of the above examples, notice how our preconceptions of the person's skill set may be rooted in a failure to understand what actually energizes the person. Look again:

- SALESPEOPLE are energized by spotting the idea that will "fly."
- ARTISTS are energized by visualizing the "how" of an initiative.
- PLANNERS are energized by spotting potentially catastrophic mistakes.
- SOLDIERS are energized by getting down to business and doing the stuff on the to-do list...and making sure that everything that is supposed to be completed is actually completed.

Each and every member of your team is energized by *something* on the short list you just read. Your job as a manager is to find out what that "something" is...get the person to start tracking activity that connects to it...and pull the team together harmoniously so that people can start sharing success stories and broadcasting their own "best practices" both before, during, and after their performance evaluations.

Bragging Rights!

This leads us to the classic mistake that a Rebel manager usually makes in dealing with any of these issues: assuming that the job description matches up with the person's primary workplace strength. Alas, job titles usually have little or nothing to do with a given person's "sweet spot."

As I say, that's the classic Rebel mistake. Here's a Flourishing manager in a nutshell: "I need to be doing a better job of pointing the right assignments to the right people. Nobody else can do that. I'm the only one who can make that happen. So starting today, I'm going to work with each of these people on my team to track activities and tasks that connect to something they do, or could do, very well."

Pull out your notebook!

Do any of the common mistakes discussed in this chapter seem relevant to your own experience as a manager?

In your notebook, select ONE of the common mistakes identified in this chapter, and make it your priority to work on over the next twenty-one days. In what specific ways do you want to make progress on dealing with this problem or challenge area over the 21 days? How will you know that you are making progress in this area?

FINALLY: Twenty-one days from today ... do you plan to be ...

... primarily an ENTHUSIASTIC manager?

... primarily a REBEL manager?

... primarily a FLOURISHING manager?

... primarily a VISIONARY manager?

To achieve your goal, what kinds of interactions would you have to have over the next twenty-one days with team members in both one-on-one and group meetings? (Who could you turn around by praising in public, for instance?) Be as specific as possible.

⇥ ⇤

Do not move on to Day 20 today,
or any other day in this book.

Complete the short written assignment (above)
in your notebook before you continue.

Celebrate Your Team

O ver the last twenty days, your team noticed that you are behaving differently, speaking differently and most importantly communicating with them more often.

You are interested in them and their ideas, their work styles and their insights. You are validating them and they feel valued.

This is a time to celebrate; a time to acknowledge yourself and your team.

Bragging Rights!

You have earned your "Bragging Rights"!

First, acknowledge yourself for your determination, commitment to grow, and create an effective, productive team.

Based on the work you have done, answer the following questions:

- What will you do in the future as a result of this process?
- What did you learn about yourself that you want to be applauded for?
- What were you willing to change and let go?
- What will you tell others about your process?

Now take your hand, reach over and pat yourself on the back. You are one of only a few managers willing to take the risk, the risk to change and become a transformed manager.

It is only when YOU take the steps, garner the courage to do things differently, reflect on your own behavior and challenge yourself to communicate and work with your team differently that you reap the rewards of a highly productive and functioning team.

Highly productive and functioning diverse teams are created; cultivated and supported by their leaders and managers.

Celebrate!

Celebrate your team members. They too have undergone changes. They didn't understand your inquisitiveness, some were down right fearful. What is he up to? Why is she suddenly so interested in me?

They played along, they followed your lead.

Now they are glad they did. Since you understand them, they can work more effectively, communicate easily and give you input (based on their strengths) and ask questions because, based on your answers, they can do a more productive, high quality job. YAHOO!

Celebrate your team in a variety of ways:

- Share your process (mentor future leaders by sharing your process).
- Open your meetings with themes (The theme – goals, for instance – give them little toy soccer balls and discuss how important goals are to the team.)
- Have walking meetings instead of sit down meet-

ings. Brainstorm by walking rather than sitting in the same room over and over.

- Give motivational books. My book "*Sometimes You Need to Kick Your Own Butt*" is a little book with a powerful punch and a perfect gift for your team.
- Provide healthy food (vegetables, fruits and sparkling water instead of donuts, coffee and candy).

Most importantly take the time to keep connected:

- Sit and chat on their turf. Ask questions about how to improve the process, what questions do clients ask about the team/product.
- Walk around and be seen – don't hide in your office.
- Keep aware of significant events in their life – a marriage, a parent's passing, a child's success – acknowledge the event with a hand written card (more powerful than a bunch of flowers).

Without them, you aren't a manager...much less a leader.

CELEBRATE...
CELEBRATE...
CELEBRATE!!!

Bragging Rights!

Pull out your notebook!

Decide how you will celebrate the team. When will it exactly happen – within the next 24 hours. Write your answers in your notebook.

+≡ ≡+

Do not move on to Day 21 today,
or any other day in this book.

Complete the short written assignment (above)
in your notebook before you continue.

It Is Time To Exercise Your Bragging Rights

The team has transformed and is moving in a positive direction. You have celebrated and evaluated your progress and changes. Now it is time for you to share your team's accomplishments with others.

While your team has gone through a transformation, so have you. You may not have noticed the changes you made, but your team has noticed. Now it is time to share your transformation and the team's transformation with others.

Pull out your notebook:

- Identify the changes that you have seen in productivity, morale, and communication.
- How has this new, better, and more effective team enhanced the services you provide?
- What improvements have you seen in processes and creativity?
- Have absenteeism, late arrivals, early departures, and water cooler breaks been reduced? How much money has that saved your department?
- Who needs to know this information?
- Why is it important to them?

As you gather your answers, you should step back and applaud yourself.

Now it is time to share your results with your superiors and struggling managers who happen to be your co-workers.

Set a time to discuss your successes and the process you

used to achieve your outcomes. Focus on why you want to communicate your success:

- To give kudos to the transformation your team experienced.

- To share the insights and growth that you experienced in your managerial skills.

- To help others on your leadership team experience the same growth you have so that your unit, division and ultimately your company receives the kudos.

AND BECAUSE...

- You worked hard on changing and deserve a pat on the back – you may not get it (especially if your boss would benefit from the techniques taught in this book), so share away and know that I am applauding you!

You can extend your experience by gifting a copy of this book to your boss and/or co-workers. Inscribe the inside with "I know that within you is a Visionary Leader" and sign your name.

During your presentation share:

- What you were like before.
- What the team was like.
- The action steps you took to change and to change the dynamics of your team:
  - Reading the book
  - Following the steps
  - Fill in what else you did _____
- The challenges you faced.
- What made you *keep on keeping on* the process.
- The changes you saw in your team.
- The changes you saw in yourself.
- When sharing the results of the transformation, point out:
  - the dollars and cents saved because your team shared cost saving processes with each other;
  - the money earned because the team found new profit centers;

- productivity increased; and

- there are indications that employee morale has improved.

This is important for you to share because, as the leader, you are encouraged to model the behavior you want to see in your staff. If you willingly share how you improved, they will be more willing to share how they have improved.

Too often, successful processes and ideas are not shared because people are afraid of what others will think of them. Have the courage to communicate the success of your team and your success as their leader. It took courage to look within and change. It took courage to do the daily workbook exercises. It takes courage to share your lessons learned.

This is your personal celebration time. You did it! No one else did it for you. It doesn't stop here. Over the next 21 days review where you were and where you are now. Each day review what you did so that you reinforce the transformation.

Be transformed.

Celebrate your transformation.

Communicate your transformation.

Encourage others to transform themselves.

ABOUT PEGINE

Pegine Echevarria, MSW, CSP is the founder and CEO of Team Pegine Inc. (TPI) a global multi-million dollar company. She is also an empowerment guru described as "audacious, bold, brilliant, clever, comical, dynamic, effective, enthusiastic, fresh, humorous, knowledgeable, perceptive, relevant, talented, vivacious, vivid, and witty!" Pegine is a leading expert on success, leadership, teamwork, and diversity.

ALSO BY PEGINE:

"Sometimes You Need To Kick Your Own Butt"

"How to be a Feisty, Focused, Fearless, Fun Female Leader"

"Breaking Through: Getting Past the Stuck Points in Your Life"
(Powerful Woman Press, 2006 – Contributing Author)

"For All Our Daughters: How Mentoring Helps Young Women and Girls Master the Art of Growing Up"

"Go Fish for Friends, Business, and Opportunities"

Bragging Rights!

She goes by her first name, Pegine (Pe-geen). If it's good enough for Oprah, Shakira, and Madonna, it's good enough for her. *New York Newsday* calls Pegine "a walking one-woman antidote to workplace cynicism." Feisty and fun, Pegine is one of 58 inductees into the prestigious *Motivational Speakers Hall of Fame* (awarded by GetMotivation. com) that includes luminaries Zig Ziglar, Dale Carnegie and Tony Robbins. She is the first Latina and one of only 8 women inducted.

The Society of Human Resource Management (SHRM) named her one of *100 Global Thought Leaders on Diversity and Inclusion*. She is an expert on **leading in a diverse world and empowering people to be leaders.** She motivates leaders in a diverse world! Pegine has presented on the stage with such notables as Maya Angelou, John Maxwell, Suze Orman, Secretary of State Hillary Rodham Clinton, President Bill Clinton as well as President Barack Obama.

Business and news shows seek her enthusiastic, bold insights including **CNN, MSNBC** and **NPR** and was the on-air expert regarding leadership, diversity and inclusion in business for **Newstalk Television.** Interviews include

The **Wall Street Journal, New York Times, Chicago Sun Times, Fortune, BusinessWeek,** and various consumer magazines.

Pegine is the author of **Sometimes You Need to Kick Your Own Butt** (one of SHRM's best-selling books) and **Lighten Up and Lead: How to be a Feisty, Fearless, Focused and Fun Female Leader** and **Rock Your World to Success** 6 CD program. She is creator of the scalable licensed training **White Guys Are Diverse Too**^(tm)**!,** which is used by Sodexo (#1 Diversity Inc. corporation), the U.S. Navy, and National Guard Bureau.

Team Pegine Inc.'s repeat clients include the U.S. Army, National Guard, The U.S. Navy, HSBC and Blue Cross Blue Shield of Florida. Pegine has testified in front of the congressionally mandated **Military Leadership Diversity Commission.**

Team Pegine, Inc. (TPI) is one of fewer than 700 businesses worldwide whose CEO was awarded the **Certified Speaking Professional** designation. The CSP is awarded to professional speaking and training business leaders after undergoing a rigorous independent audit for expertise, eloquence, enterprise and ethics. The audit, conducted by the National Speakers Association, included interviewing and surveying clients, evaluating five years of documented business practices including ethics, customer service, client ROI, financial review, marketing as well as presentation style.

She holds a Masters in Social Work in group and organizational behavior, and has received numerous awards for her work on diversity and leadership.

Pegine was a gang member, president of a direct sales company, owned two businesses in Spain which she sold at a profit (all before the age of 23), performs stand-up comedy to reduce stress, and rides a motorcycle.

TEAM PEGINE

Team Pegine, Inc. (TPI) was founded in 1996, by Pegine Echevarria, MSW, CSP. Team Pegine, Inc. (TPI) manifests success in a diverse world for our clients. Team Pegine, Inc. is a global, multi-million dollar think-tank company. TPI provides training, event planning and organizational development for clients such as The Department of Defense, US Army, US Navy, US Marines, US Air Force, The US Coast Guard, Department of Homeland Security, Intel, Sodexo, Newell Rubbermaid, and Unilever. Her company produced and managed the Memorial Day Commemoration of the 50th Anniversary of the Vietnam War at the Vietnam Veterans Memorial attended by The President, and 10,000 people. TPI also provides cultural role players for military leadership exercises that serve thousands of officers.

Go to www.TeamPegine.com to learn more

Sign up for Pegine's leadership newsletter and received a free book to build your leadership persona and access more information at www.Pegine.com